71 Creative Bible Story Projects

by Helen W. Gramelsbach

illustrated by Romilda Dilley

STANDARD PUBLISHING
Cincinnati, Ohio

2103

Library of Congress Catalog Card Number: 82-61178

ISBN: 0-87239-607-X

© 1983 by The STANDARD PUBLISHING COMPANY, Cincinnati, Ohio.
Division of STANDEX INTERNATIONAL CORPORATION.
Printed in U.S.A.

CONTENTS

HINTS AND HELPS

Patterns

In order to use the patterns in this book you will need tracing paper (or some type of thin paper) and carbon paper or a soft black pencil. Lay the tracing paper over the pattern you plan to use and copy with a sharp pencil. Place this tracing over the good paper, with a sheet of carbon paper between. Or, you may simply turn over your tracing and use a soft black pencil to go over your lines on the back of your tracing. Then place this directly on the good paper and proceed to go over your lines with a sharp pencil. This will give you a suitable copy. If you must make several copies of an item, trace your pattern onto lightweight cardboard, cut this out, and draw around the cardboard pattern onto good paper, making as many copies as you need.

How to Enlarge a Pattern

There may be times when you want to enlarge a pattern. Divide the original pattern into 1-inch squares. Divide a larger piece of paper into 2-inch, 3-inch, or 4-inch squares, depending on how much you want to enlarge the pattern. Then copy the original pattern square by square onto the larger sheet.

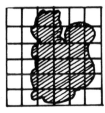 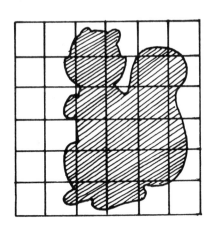

Construction Paper

The construction paper called for throughout the book is the 9-inch by 12-inch size, unless otherwise indicated. Although certain colors are called for, feel free to use whatever colors you have available or prefer.

Any paper projects you wish to preserve should be covered with clear adhesive-backed plastic. This is a simple process that is well worth the small expense and effort required.

Post-It Note Tape

This tape, which can be purchased wherever office or school supplies are sold, is a tape that can be used again and again. Because of this, it is suitable to put on the backs of paper-doll clothes that will be put off and on so many times. Glue the plain side of the tape to the back of the clothing so that the sticky side will be toward the doll.

Aqua Podge

Aqua Podge is a decoupage liquid that can be purchased at a craft-supply shop. You may substitute another brand of decoupaging liquid for this when called for.

Play Dough

To make a dough that will stay usable for many weeks, mix 1 cup flour, ½ cup salt, and 2 teaspoons cream of tartar in a sucepan. (Do not omit the cream of tartar.) Add 1 cup water, 1 tablespoon cooking oil, several drops of oil of wintergreen (optional) and food coloring. Cook, stirring, for three minutes or until mixture pulls away from the pan. Knead immediately. Store in an airtight container. This recipe makes enough dough for about six children.

Bread-Dough Clay

The basic recipe for this quick-drying dough is: 1 slice of bread (without crusts—may be slightly dry), 1 tablespoon of glycerine, and 1 teaspoon powdered tempera paint. Break the bread into small pieces, add the glycerine and tempera, and work with your fingers until a dough forms. Store in a plastic bag in the refrigerator. Since this dough dries rapidly, give each child only enough to make one item at a time.

OLD TESTAMENT PROJECTS

Creation Circle

Genesis 1:1-27

Materials needed:
Construction paper—black and white
Felt-tip pens or tempera paints
Brass paper fastener
Acetate—clear
Tagboard
Yarn
Glue

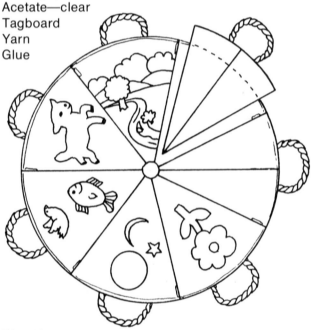

Directions:
Make a cardboard wedge-shape guide from the pattern on page 18. Cut a circle from tagboard and one from the acetate, each 7⅝ inches in diameter. Glue two pieces of black construction paper together. Cut seven wedge-shape pieces from tagboard and seven from white construction paper. Glue tagboard and paper wedges together. Draw a line down the middle of the first one and color half black and half yellow. Divide the second one and color half blue and half green-blue. Trace and color a flower on the third; sun, moon, and star on the fourth; a bird and a fish on the fifth; a lamb on the sixth; seventh, the peaceful scene on the pattern page. On the backs of each wedge glue a 3-inch yarn loop. Also print this information (on the backs of the appropriate wedges): 1—Light and Darkness; 2—Sky and Waters; 3—Plants; 4—Sun, Moon, Stars; 5—Fish and birds; 6—Animals and Man; 7—God rested.

On the tagboard circle mark off the seven sections, using the wedge-shape pattern. Number the wedges from one to seven with large numbers. Now place the tagboard circle with the acetate circle over it, on the black paper. Hold in place with the paper fastener. Put staples through both circles at the end of each dividing line to separate sections of the circle. Insert finished wedges in their sections.

Use this as a visual for a lesson on creation, or place it in a learning center (with pieces removed) and leave directions for reading the Scripture and placing the wedges in their proper places. The activity will be self-correcting since the information is on the backs of the wedges. Encourage the children not to look at this until they have completed the assignment.

Dove

Genesis 8:8-12; Matthew 3:13-17

Materials needed:
Construction paper—white and green
Felt—white (optional)
Cotton balls—6 (optional)
Crayons or felt-tip pens
Thread
Glue

Directions

Paper Dove: From pattern on page 18, cut two birds and two wings from white paper, and two leaves from green. Glue bodies together, inserting a 20-inch thread where indicated. Do not glue tails or beaks together. Color beak and eyes. Glue wings where indicated and attach one on each side of body. Glue leaves together and glue between beaks. Glue a small tag of paper to end of thread and hang dove where he can "fly."

Felt Dove: Use the dove pattern to cut two felt birds and two felt wings. Place a thin line of white glue around the edge of one dove, leaving a 2-inch space at the bottom to add filler. Place second dove over glue and press together. Allow plenty of drying time. Now stuff with cotton, about six cotton balls spread out, or cotton batting. When bird is stuffed evenly, glue space at bottom and allow to dry. Glue wings in place. Add a 20-inch thread at top to hang up dove.

Noah's Floating Zoo

Genesis 6:13–8:22

Materials needed:

Construction paper—various colors
Crayons, felt-tip pens, or tempera paints
Styrofoam tray (small)
Glue

Directions:

Using patterns on page 19, cut ark and decks from brown construction paper and roof from red. Fold roof and glue over fold of ark. Fold flaps up at bottom of ark and glue to Styrofoam tray, 1 inch apart. (Tray may have color added if you wish.) Now glue decks to sides of ark. Glue slivers of yellow construction paper to floor of ark.

Trace two of each animal and of Noah on appropriate shades of construction paper. Cut out and glue together, leaving lower legs and feet apart so figures can stand. Add details with felt-tip pens.

Noah's Ark Pop-Up

Materials needed:

Construction paper—variety of colors
Tagboard
Glue
Felt-tip pens
Plasti-Tak

Directions

To make base, glue two pieces of tan or green construction paper together. Fold across middle and set aside. Cut and assemble ark according to directions given for ark above. Glue ark ½ inch on either side of crease of base. Leave tops of decks open so figures can be inserted.

Make animals according to directions above, gluing animals' feet and legs together, except for animals that will be placed inside ark.

Cut eight supports and glue together and fold to make four double-strength supports.

To assemble, glue cows and donkey to inside of

ark, feet apart. Glue monkey to roof. Glue A ends of supports to ark as shown and D ends to base. Glue animals to C sections and supports. Dove can be held on roof or in Noah's hand with a bit of Plasti-Tak.

Have visual folded shut as you begin story, then open, and ark and animals will pop up. If you prefer, make two of each animal to indicate pairs. Glue one dove to roof and place other dove in Noah's hand.

The Sign of God's Promise

Genesis 9:12-17

Materials needed:

Construction paper—gray (2), white
Tagboard
Crayons or tempera paints
Glue
Brass paper fastener

Directions:

Cut rainbow from tagboard, using pattern on page 18. Color with crayons or tempera paints. Cut tab, 4 inches by ⅝ inch, fold in half and glue together, then glue on back of rainbow. Cut one sheet of gray construction paper in half and fasten

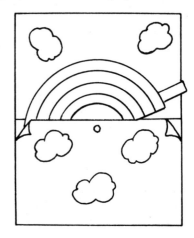

rainbow as shown in sketch. Glue around edge of this half and place on bottom half of second sheet of gray paper. Leave corners unglued as indicated. Glue second half of gray to the top of large sheet. Cut clouds from white paper and glue in place.

When using as a visual, rainbow remains out of sight until you are ready for it.

Jacob's Dream

Genesis 28:10-22

Materials needed:
Construction paper—red, white, black or navy
Gold or silver stars
Glue
Tempera paints or felt-tip pens
angel pattern - p. 21

Directions:
Cut six or eight angels from white construction paper. Glue them together by two's, leaving the wings and corners of skirts unglued. Add color to both sides. Cut the ladder from red construction paper and glue only the rungs to the black or navy paper. Add gold or silver stars to background. Angels may be placed on the ladder by slipping skirt corners and/or wings beneath ladder side-pieces.

Joseph and His Beautiful Coat

Genesis 37:2-4

Materials needed:
Tagboard
Crayons, felt-tip pens, or tempera paints
Chenille wire
Glue

Striped fabric
Yarn (optional)

Directions:
Cut two figures from tagboard using pattern on page 22. Bend a 12-inch chenille wire in half and glue on one figure, allowing 1 inch to extend below each foot. Glue other figure over chenille wire and allow to dry. Color with crayons, felt-tip pens, or tempera paints. Cut two stands, each 2 inches by 3¼ inches. Punch holes in one piece to fit feet of figure. Push extending wires through holes and bend one forward and the other back. Glue other stand to bottom of this. Allow to dry.

To make garment, copy pattern on page 22. Fold fabric and lay pattern on fold. Cut out and either stitch or glue seam. Place garment on doll and tie with a strip of the fabric or a length of yarn. If you prefer, Joseph can be a paper doll with paper clothing. See directions for Samuel paper doll.

Joseph Is Kind to His Brothers

Genesis 42

Materials needed:
Construction paper—gray or brown, and contrasting color
Cardboard or tagboard
Popcorn (unpopped)
Felt-tip pen—black
Silver crayon or foil
Chenille Wire
Yarn
Glue

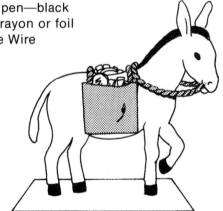

Directions:

Using donkey pattern (page 23), cut two donkeys out of gray or brown construction paper. Draw details with black felt-tip pen. Glue figures together, inserting one 3-inch piece of chenille wire in front and one piece in back legs. Leave 1-inch ends of wire below feet. Cut two bases, 3½ inches by 2½ inches. Punch holes to match with feet and insert chenille wire ends in holes, bending wires in opposite directions. Glue other base on bottom, over exposed wires. Cut two saddlebags from contrasting shade of paper. Fold and glue on sides, inserting small pieces of yarn in seams to connect bags. Place saddlebags over donkey's back and add glue beneath yarn. Cut coins from cardboard or tagboard and color with silver crayon, or cover with foil. Put corn and coins in saddlebags. Cut 6 inches of yarn and tie ends together. Cut a slit for donkey's mouth and insert yarn rein.

Baby in a Basket

Exodus 2:1-10

Materials needed:

Small Styrofoam tray
Tagboard
Felt-tip pens—permanent ink
Brass paper fastener
Cloth—about 10-inch square

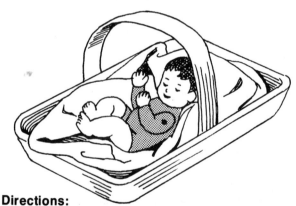

Directions:

Cut two babies and two arms (patterns on page 23) from tagboard and glue bodies together and arms together. Color baby and arm. Attach arm with the brass paper fastener. Color bottom of "basket" with permanent-ink pen. Cut a handle from tagboard, 11 inches long and ¾ inch wide. Color and staple or tape to basket. Wrap baby in blanket and put his little arm out to hold blanket in place. Put in the basket. Have a large pan of water to float basket in as you tell the story.

The Burning Bush

Exodus 3:1-6

Materials needed:

Acetate—clear
Felt-tip pens—permanent ink
Masking tape
Black thread

Directions:

Trace pattern from page 24 onto a small piece of paper. Place clear acetate over pattern. Secure both paper and acetate to table with masking tape. Color with permanent-ink felt-tip pens. (Note the color key on the pattern page.) Make a heavy black outline as indicated on pattern. Cut around bush when coloring is finished. Attach a length of black thread to top and hang in window. This can be used as a visual or a craft with the story about Moses.

Crossing the Red Sea

Exodus 14

Materials needed:

Construction paper—tan (12 inches by 18 inches)
Brass paper fastener
Acetate—blue (2 sheets)
Crayons, felt-tip pens, or tempera paints
Tan ribbon (optional)

Directions:

Mount large paper on cardboard to strengthen it. If you do not have paper this size, use two sheets of standard-size paper and glue to the cardboard. Trace fish and other sea life here and there on the paper and color. (See page 24 for patterns.) Cut a 2½-inch slit in the board, about 1½ inches from the top. Cut two strips of tan paper, 2 inches wide by 18 inches long. Trace some of the Israelite figures on one strip (using about 9 inches of strip) and color. Next, add Egyptian figures at lower part of strip, using about 7 inches of strip (leave 2 inches blank

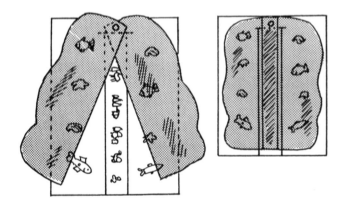

in between Israelites and Egyptians). Glue strips together securely and thread through hole in board. Bring strips togehter in back and glue other ends securely, leaving some slack in the strip. This will allow strip to be pulled round and round.

Now cut two pieces (see sketch) from blue plastic for water. Overlap these pieces and fasten at top with a brass paper fastener. As story is told, have the blank part of strip showing beneath water. Then at proper time, have sea roll back and move Israelites through dry land. Then Egyptians will follow and the sea can be closed over them.

If you prefer, use a satin ribbon in place of the strips of paper. Cut and glue figures to ribbon. This will move more easily than the paper strip.

Water for God's People

Exodus 17

Materials needed:
Gray clay (a moist type such
  as Plast-i-Clay)
Large shallow pan (or many
  small Styrofoam trays)
Tempera paint—
  gray

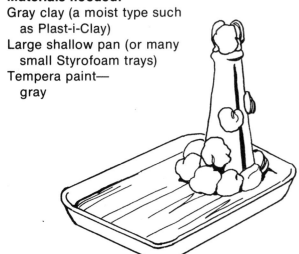

Directions:
If you are preparing this as a visual for the Bible story given above, use a large bottle. Paint it with gray tempera paint, a latex base paint, or enamel. Punch several holes in the bottle—one near the bottom, others here and there. Cover holes with clay "rocks" to prevent water from leaking. Also add clay here and there to make bottle resemble a large rock. Place bottle at one end of a shallow pan large enough to hold the water contained in the bottle. As you tell the story, you can release the water by uncovering the holes in the bottle.

If this is a craft project, punch one hole near bottom and another about 1 inch from bottom. Let the children color their Styrofoam trays with blue crayon. Set their "rocks" at one end of the trays with the holes facing the opposite end. Add no more water than the trays hold!

The Promised Land

Number 13

Materials needed:
Acetate—clear
Construction paper—black
Felt-tip pens—permanent ink
Glue
Dark thread
Masking tape

Directions:
Cut acetate to 5 inches by 6 inches. Make a copy of the design from the pattern on page 25. Place the piece of acetate over the pattern and fasten to table with masking tape. Have a selection of permanent-ink felt-tip pens ready. Color in the various sections. When this is dry, use a black pen to outline each section. Cut two frames from black construction paper. Make these 6½ inches by 7½ inches (outside measurement) , and 1 inch wide. Glue the acetate between the two frames. Attach a short piece of black thread at center top and hang in a window.

Ram's Horn

Materials needed:
Cardboard rod from pants hanger
Newspaper
Transparent tape
Scraps of trim (optional)

Directions:
Cut a cardboard rod from a pants hanger to measure 8 inches. Bend gently in the center to form the curve in the ram's horn. Roll this rod in a double sheet of newspaper, allowing it to be tight around one end where the trumpet is blown, and spreading out at the other end. Tape around the curve to hold newspaper in place. Trim the mouth end even with the rod and glue to rod. Trim the large end to about 5 inches from the end of the rod. Now roll the horn in a large piece of heavy aluminum foil, tucking in the ends. Mash foil firmly around the curved area. Trim the large end and middle of curve with scraps of trim if you wish.

Use this ram's horn with the story of the fall of Jericho (Joshua 6) or the story of Gideon and his men (Judges 7), or any other story requiring a ram's horn.

The Longest Day

Joshua 10:1-15

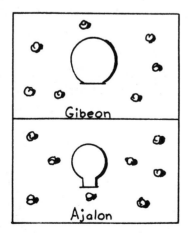

Materials needed:
Construction paper—yellow, gray, blue
Glue
Thin plastic (dry-cleaning bag)

Directions:
Cut two yellow suns and two gray moons using patterns on page 25. Glue suns together and moons together. Divide blue construction paper in the middle with a pen line. Print "Gibeon" at top and "Ajalon" at bottom. Cut slits for sun and for moon. Glue second sheet of construction paper to back of first one. Glue only around edges. If you want to add hailstones, cut pieces of thin plastic about 4 inches by 8 inches. Tie two or three knots in the center and trim off ends. Place generous dots of glue here and there on the top paper and press the plastic knots in place. Allow to dry thoroughly. Let the children tell you where to place the moon and the sun.

Ruth, Who Loved God

Book of Ruth

Materials needed:
Acetate—red
Dark thread
Dried grasses
Aqua Podge

Directions:
Cut a heart out of the clear red acetate, using the pattern on page 25. Punch a hole where indicated and attach a dark thread for hanging. Add a paper tag at the end of the thread. (Children can wind their threads around the tags to keep them from tangling on the way home!) Cut grasses and tie with a thread to resemble a sheaf of wheat. Coat one side of the heart with the Aqua Podge, place the sheaf of grass on the heart, and allow to dry. Give heart and grass a second coat of Aqua Podge, making sure that the dried grass is coated thoroughly. Hang when dry.

Gideon and the Fleece

Judges 6:36-40

Materials needed:
Quilt batting or roll of cotton
Glue
White cloth (optional)

Directions:
Using the pattern on page 26, cut the fleece out of the cotton batting. If you do not have batting, cut fleece from a scrap of white cloth (an old sheet will do) and glue on cotton, from a roll, or use cotton balls. You may want to use one of the stand-up dolls for Gideon. (See Joseph, page 9.)

Explain to the children that the wool (fleece) of the sheep is cut in one piece, so that it retains the shape of the animal. This does not hurt the sheep at all.

Samuel Paper Doll

1 Samuel 1:27, 28; 2:18, 19

Materials needed:
Tagboard
Construction paper
Crayons, felt-tip pens, or tempera paints
Scraps of decorations (optional)
Outing flannel, felt (optional)
Glue

Directions:
Cut paper doll (pattern on page 22) from tagboard and add color. Cut several garments from construction paper. Let the children decorate with crayons or felt-tip pens. Glue several pieces of Post-It Note tape to backs of clothing.

If you prefer, glue a piece of outing flannel over dolls' undergarment and cut outer garments from felt. Glue scraps of braid or rick rack trim to garments. These clothes will stay in place without tape.

David Spares Saul's Life

1 Samuel 26

Materials needed:
Cardboard rods from pants hangers (2)
Tagboard
Craft stick
Glue
Gilt paint (non-toxic)
Masking tape
Plastic aspirin bottle

Directions:
Cut two spearheads from tagboard with pattern from page 26. Glue spearheads together with one end of a rod in between. Glue craft stick halfway into the opposite end of rod. Let dry. Put rods together by gluing rest of craft stick inside end of second rod. When dry, paint with gilt paint.

To make cruse or jug, twist a chenille wire around the top of the plastic aspirin bottle to form a handle. Cover the entire bottle and handle with a self-drying clay dough. Paint to look like a pottery vessel.

Use the spear and cruse with the above story, or as an illustration when speaking of Bible-times equipment.

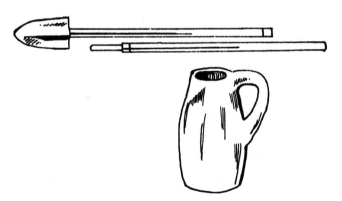

Elijah's Raven

1 Kings 17:1-7

Materials needed:

Construction paper—black, scrap of red
Glue
Black thread
Crayons or paint

Directions:

Cut two ravens out of black construction paper, and two pieces of meat out of the red paper. (See page 26 for patterns.) Glue raven pieces together, inserting 20-inch piece of thread as indicated. Glue meat between raven's beaks. Add raven's eyes with white crayon or paint. Hang in a window or suspend from the ceiling. Use as a visual or a craft.

Elijah on Mt. Carmel

1 Kings 18:20-40

Materials needed:

Construction paper—dark green, red, gray, brown, light blue
Yarn—dark green
Tempera paint
Glue

Directions:

Cut twenty-four rocks from gray paper. (See page 24 for all patterns.) Use half of these to form an altar in the lower half of one sheet of green paper. Cut two sacrifices from red paper. Glue one of these on this altar. In second sheet of green paper, punch one hole 1 inch from top and one hole in lower half of paper, where altar will be placed. Glue rest of rocks together to form an altar. Place this over lower hole and glue only around edges. Also glue sacrifice to altar. Paint water around base of altar

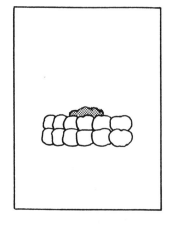

with blue paint. Cut from brown paper and glue four barrels around edge as shown in sketch. Cut flame from red paper and add yellow highlights with tempera paints. Glue this to middle of 20-inch piece of green yarn. Thread yarn through holes with flame on top. Cut sky from blue paper and glue this around edges to top of paper. Glue green sheets together, back to back.

As you tell the story, start with the plain altar. Then turn paper over. Keep flame under "sky" until you tell about the fire coming down from Heaven to consume the sacrifice, the rocks, and the water. Then pull yarn, and flame will come down from "Heaven."

Sheep Without a Shepherd

1 Kings 22:1-37

Materials needed:

Construction paper—green
Clear adhesive backed plastic
Tempera paints

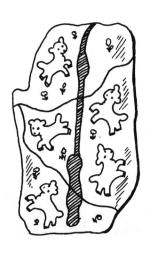

Directions:

Trace pattern of map (page 27) on a piece of light green construction paper. Paint lambs and water with the paints. When dry, cover map with the plastic to preserve it. Cut on dotted lines into three pieces. Let the children put the puzzle together and take it apart to show how the people of Israel were to be as sheep without a shepherd.

Use this in a learning center. Have a Bible for the children to read the story. Have a set of two or three simple questions for them to answer. These could be true/false. Cover questions with the plastic and let the children circle the correct answer with a wipe-off crayon. This activity can be used again and again.

Elijah and Elisha Cross the Jordan

2 Kings 2:1-8

Materials needed:
Construction paper—green, blue, scrap of color
Crayons, felt-tip pens, or tempera paints
Clear adhesive-backed plastic
Brass paper fastener
Glue

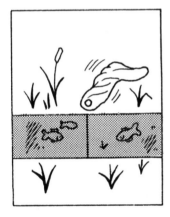

Directions:

Cut two pieces of blue construction paper, 7 inches by 2¼ inches. Score and fold each piece 1 inch from end. Trace fish and objects on strips and color. Cover strips with pieces of clear adhesive-backed plastic, leaving the 1-inch tabs. Trace plants, etc., on green paper and color. Trace and cut robe from white or other color. Glue 1-inch tabs of blue strips to backs of green so ends of blue meet in middle of page. Fasten robe above strips of water with brass paper fastener as shown. Use as a visual, "striking" water with robe and turning back water at the proper time in the story.

Elijah Goes to Heaven

2 Kings 2:9-11

Materials needed:
Construction paper—dark blue, white
Crayons, felt tip pens, or tempera paints
Yarn—dark blue

Directions:

Trace the picture of Elijah and the chariot and horses (pattern on page 28) onto white construction paper. Color the picture. Punch two holes in the dark blue paper, as shown. Glue the center section of an 18-inch piece of dark blue yarn across the picture. Optional: Cut a second piece of paper to mount on the back of the picture for strength. When dry, thread yarn through the holes. Finish yarn ends with small paper tags. Cut cloud from white paper and glue at top and side edges to background as shown in sketch. Elijah will now "go to Heaven" by sliding the picture under the cloud. Glue a second piece of construction paper under background for durability. Make sure yarn can be moved freely.

Bible-Times Furniture

Materials needed:
Tagboard
Glue
Crayons
Scrap of orange paper
Wooden bead

Directions:

Cut the furniture from tagboard and follow directions on patterns (page 29) for folding. Glue the two headboards and the back of the chair in place. When dry, color with brown crayon. The lamp is

made from a wooden bead with a scrap of orange paper for the flame. This furniture can be used to illustrate the story of Elisha's special room (2 Kings 4:8-10), or used to represent any Bible-times home. Let the children build a Bible-times house out of blocks and use the furniture to play with in their house. Or make a house out of a cardboard box and let them play with this, pretending to be certain Bible characters.

Naaman

2 Kings 5:1-14

Materials needed:
Styrofoam tray
Crayons
Brass paper fastener
Craft stick
Acetate—any color

Directions:
    Cut figure of Naaman (page 21) from the Styrofoam tray. Color heavily with crayons. Cut two of his garments from the acetate. Drill a small hole in one end of the craft stick. Use the paper fastener to secure Naaman's garments on front and back and fasten through the craft stick as shown in the sketch. Have a pan of water when you tell the story and allow the children to take turns dunking Naaman seven times. They'll remember through doing!

Jonah and the Big Fish

Book of Jonah

Materials needed:
Construction paper—black, red
Tagboard
Glue
Yarn
Crayons, felt-tip pens, or tempera paints

Directions:
    Cut two black fish and two red ones (patterns on page 29). Glue a red fish to each black one. (Make sure one set faces left and one set faces right.) Then glue the red sides together, leaving an opening around the mouth large enough to slip Jonah inside. Add a white eye and red around the mouth. Cut two figures of Jonah from tagboard. Glue these together, inserting one end of a 5-inch piece of yarn between figures. Color figure. Knot the end of yarn. Place Jonah, feet first, inside fish, letting yarn hang out fish's mouth. If you are making this for a visual, you will probably want to enlarge the patterns.

Daniel and His Friends

Daniel 1

Materials needed:
Construction paper—any color
Tagboard
Glue
Felt-tip pens or tempera paints
Heavy-duty foil
Paper cups—3 inches tall (2)
Plastic dry-cleaning bag
Clay*

Glue
Crayons, felt-tip pens, or tempera paints

Directions:

Cut the four figures from tagboard, using the patterns on pages 27 and 28. Color the figures. Cut free-form flames from red construction paper. Cut these about 9½ inches wide and 4 inches high at peaks. Make three folds in flames, then add yellow color. Place glue on bottom and sides of flames and glue to orange sheet, about 1½ inches from bottom. Allow flames to "pleat" where they were folded to give them a slight 3-D effect. Cut a piece of black paper, 9 inches by 2½ inches. Put glue on bottom and sides of this and place at bottom, over flames. Figures can now be slipped behind flames and removed easily.

Directions:

Cut two plates from construction paper and two from tagboard, all 5 inches in diameter. Glue a paper plate to each tagboard plate. Decorate plates with felt-tip pens or paints. Model food out of bread-dough clay or any self-hardening clay. When food is thoroughly dry, color with the pens or paints. Glue to plates. Cut the cups down to 1½ inches tall. Cover cups with the foil. Twist or fold a scrap to make the handle. Staple or glue in place. Make stem and base of goblet with the extra foil by twisting and flattening into shape. Stuff each container with a bit of plastic from a dry-cleaning bag. (Watch this around children!) Tint the "wine" with a red felt-tip pen. Glue cup and goblet to plates.

(*See recipe on page 5 for bread dough.)

In the Fiery Furnace

Daniel 3

Materials needed:
Tagboard
Construction paper—black, red, orange

Esther Paper Doll

Materials needed:
Tagboard
Construction paper—various colors
Glue
Gold glitter
Cotton ball
Felt-tip pens or tempera paints
Fancy wrapping paper (optional)

Directions:

Cut paper doll out of tagboard, using pattern on page 30. Color with the pens or paints. Cut robe and crown from construction paper. Glue tabs of crown together. Add glue to crown and dip into glitter (or sprinkle on glitter). Unroll cotton ball and use it to trim robe. Make dresses using fancy wrapping paper or use construction paper and decorate with glitter, etc. Add Post-It Note tape to backs of all garments.

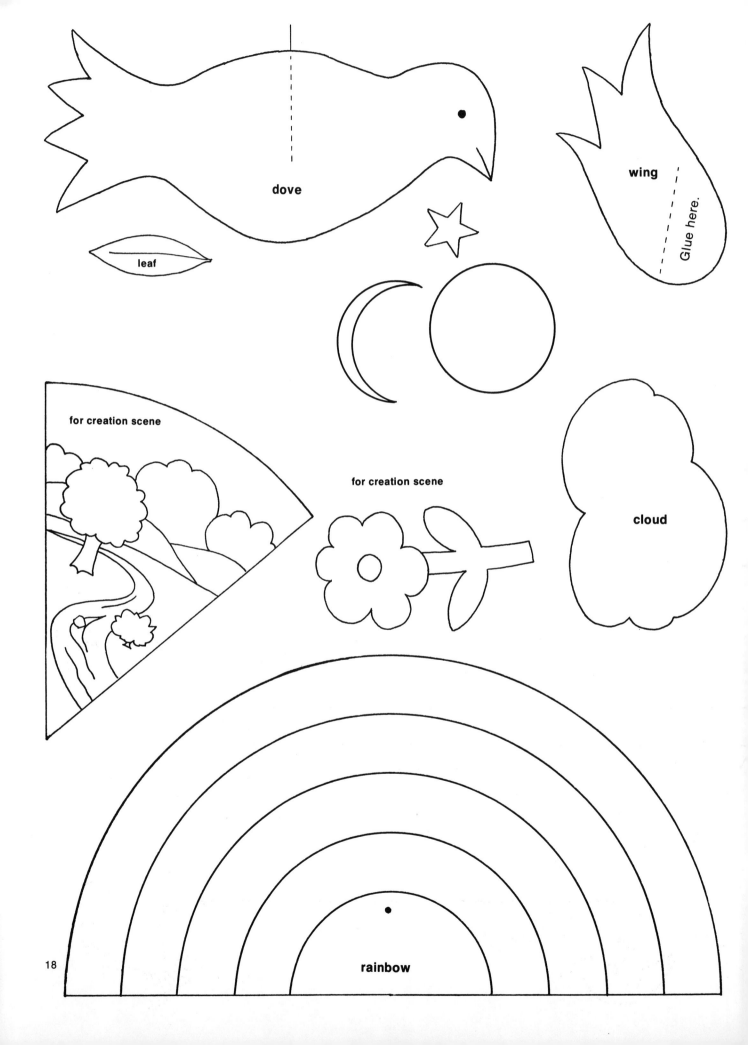

dove

wing

Glue here.

leaf

for creation scene

for creation scene

cloud

rainbow

18

Place on fold of paper.

Fold back and
glue to ark.

A

ARK
Cut 1.

B

Fold down.

C

Noah

Fold under and
glue to ground.

D

Fold up.

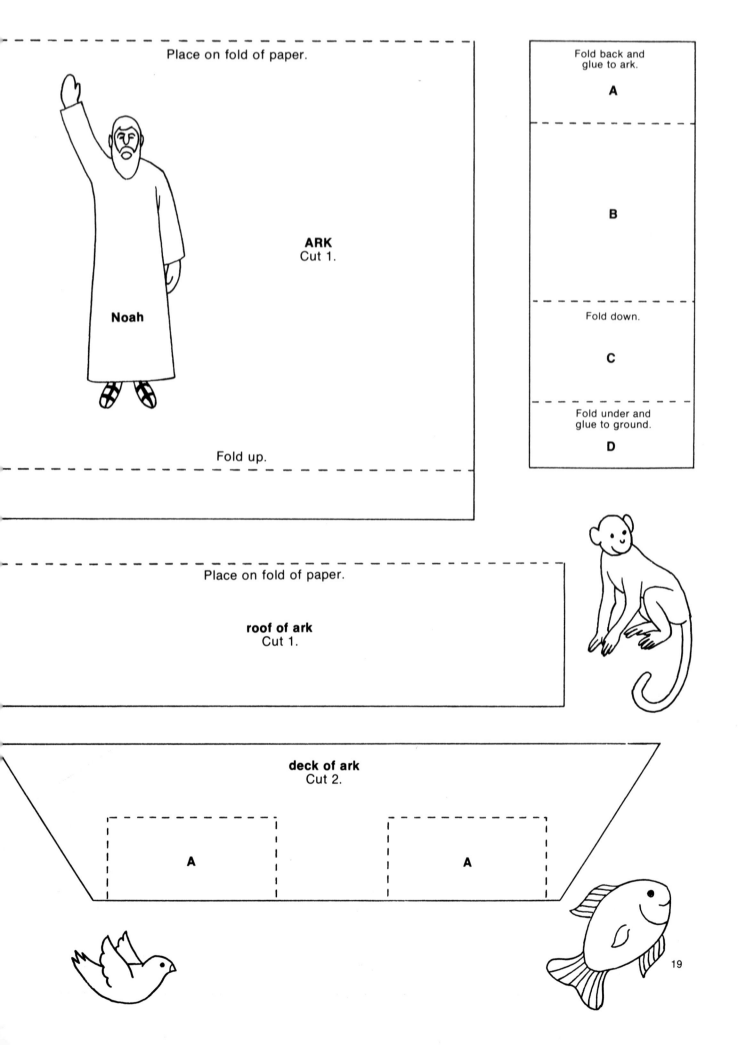

Place on fold of paper.

roof of ark
Cut 1.

deck of ark
Cut 2.

A   **A**

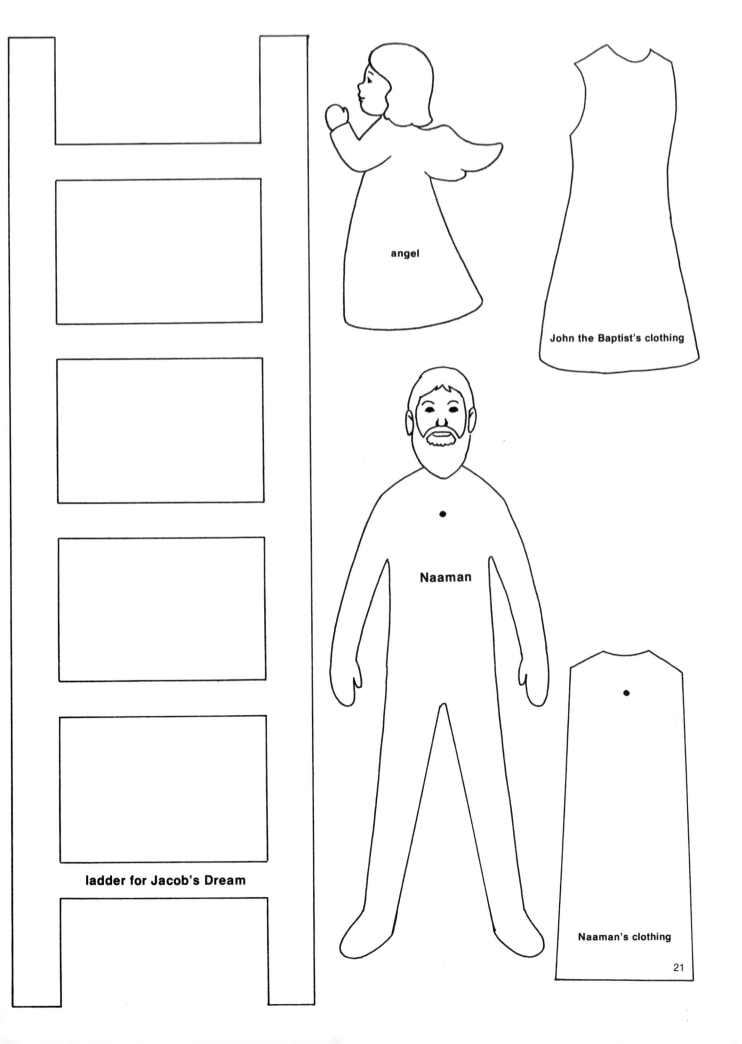

angel

John the Baptist's clothing

Naaman

ladder for Jacob's Dream

Naaman's clothing

21

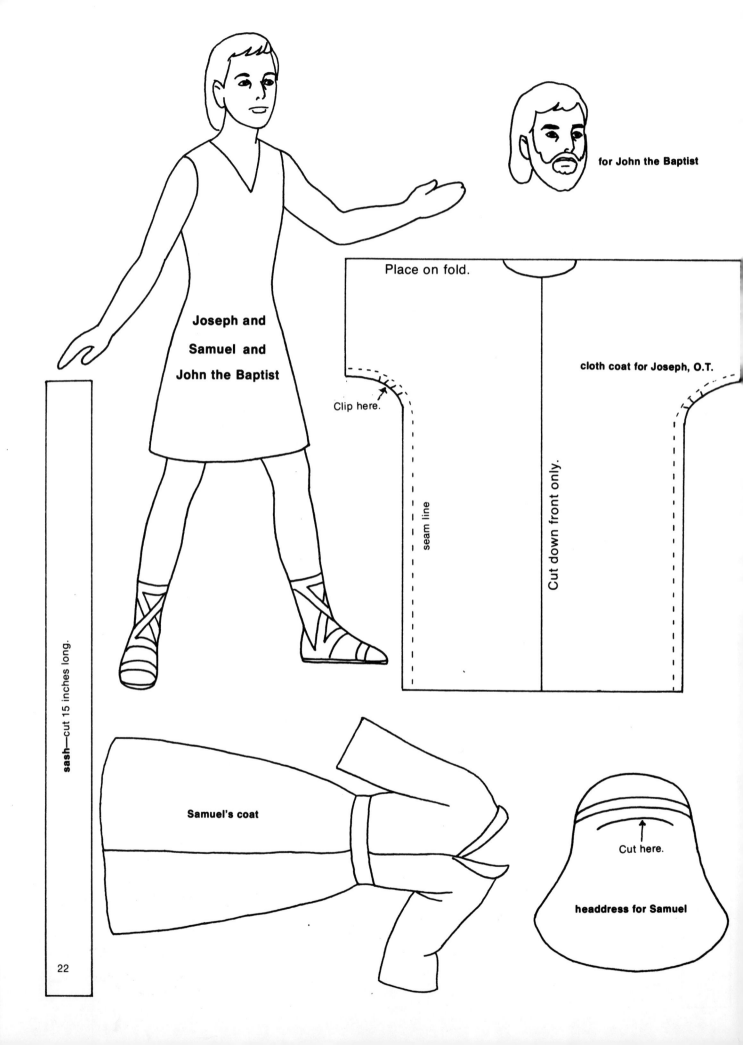

for John the Baptist

Joseph and
Samuel and
John the Baptist

Place on fold.

cloth coat for Joseph, O.T.

Clip here.

seam line

Cut down front only.

sash—cut 15 inches long.

Samuel's coat

Cut here.

headdress for Samuel

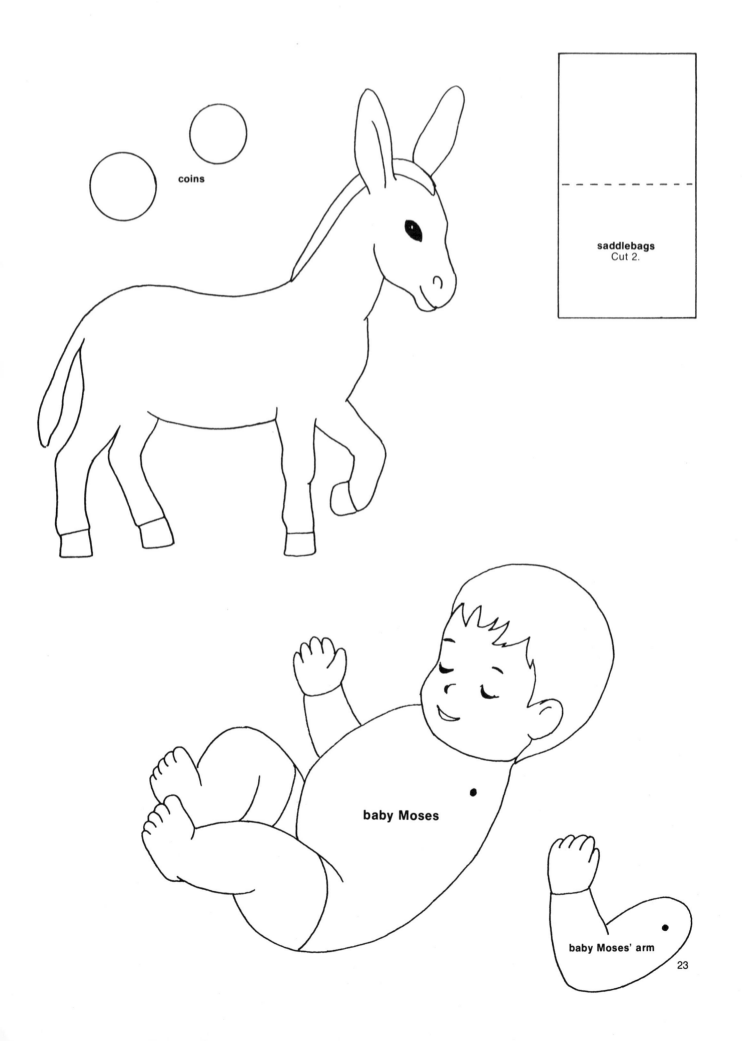

coins

saddlebags
Cut 2.

baby Moses

baby Moses' arm

23

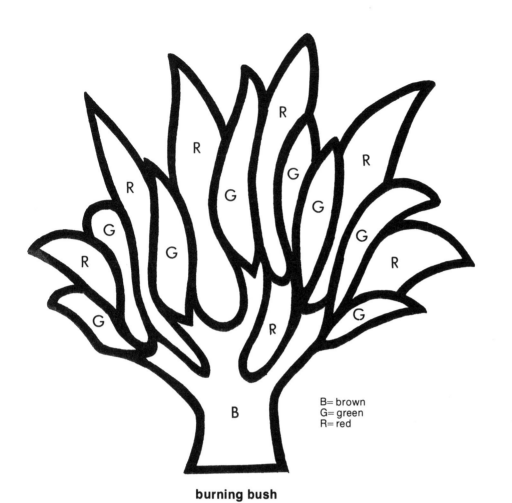

B= brown
G= green
R= red

burning bush

for Crossing the Red Sea

Israelites

Egyptians

24

for Elijah on Mt. Carmel

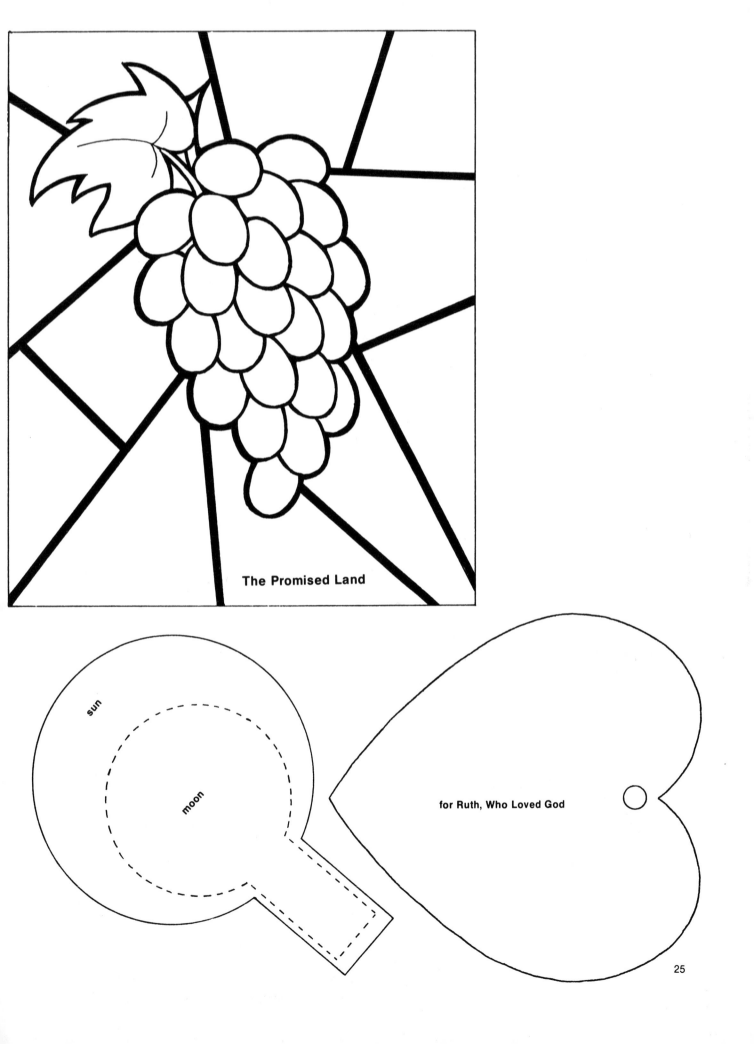

The Promised Land

sun

moon

for Ruth, Who Loved God

25

Gideon's fleece

spearhead

meat

raven

26

figure for fiery furnace

Elijah's cloak

for Sheep Without a Shepherd

27

cloud

Elijah and the
chariot of fire

figures for fiery furnace

28

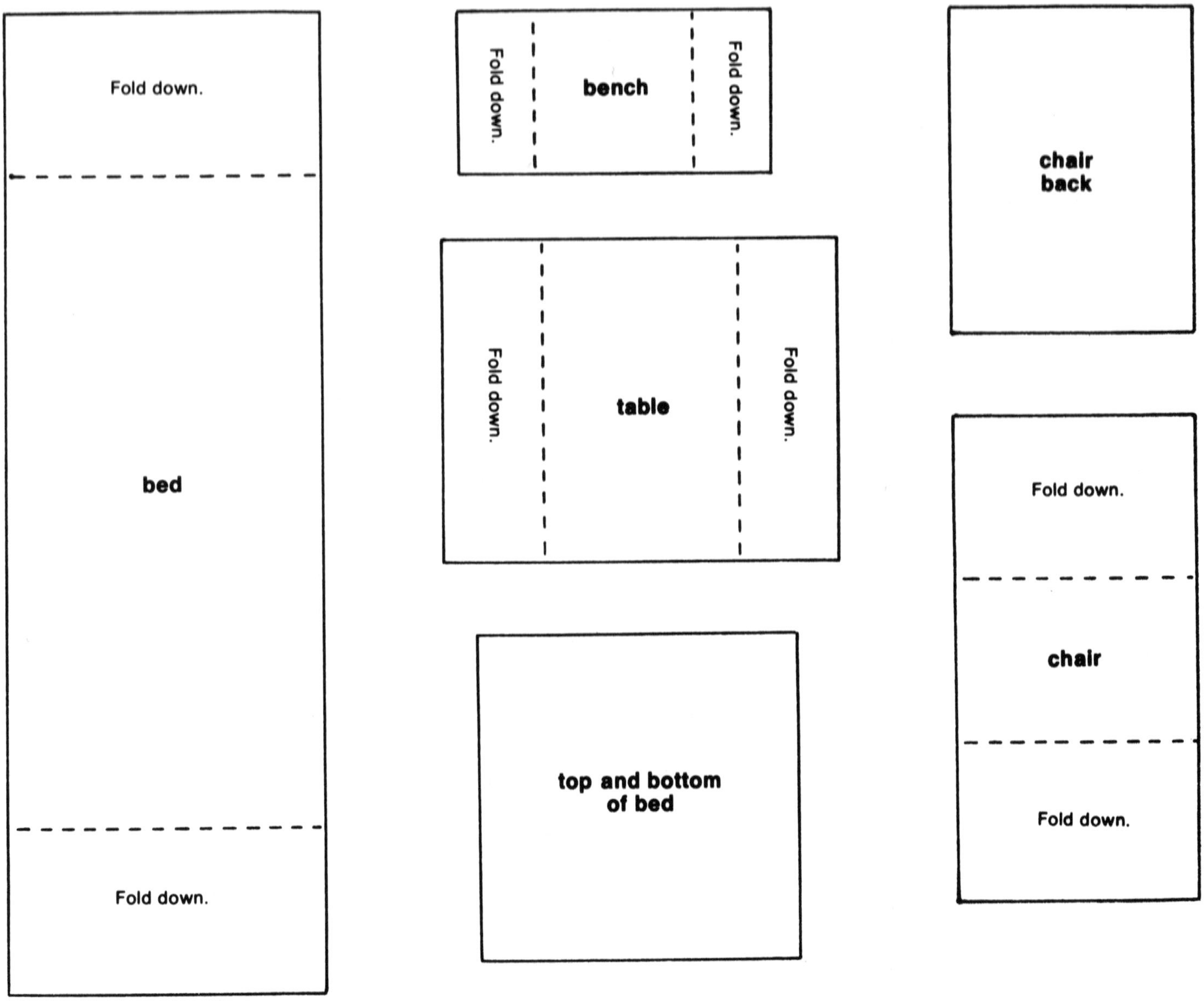

Fold down.

bench

Fold down.

Fold down.

chair
back

bed

table

Fold down.

Fold down.

Fold down.

chair

Fold down.

top and bottom
of bed

Jonah

29

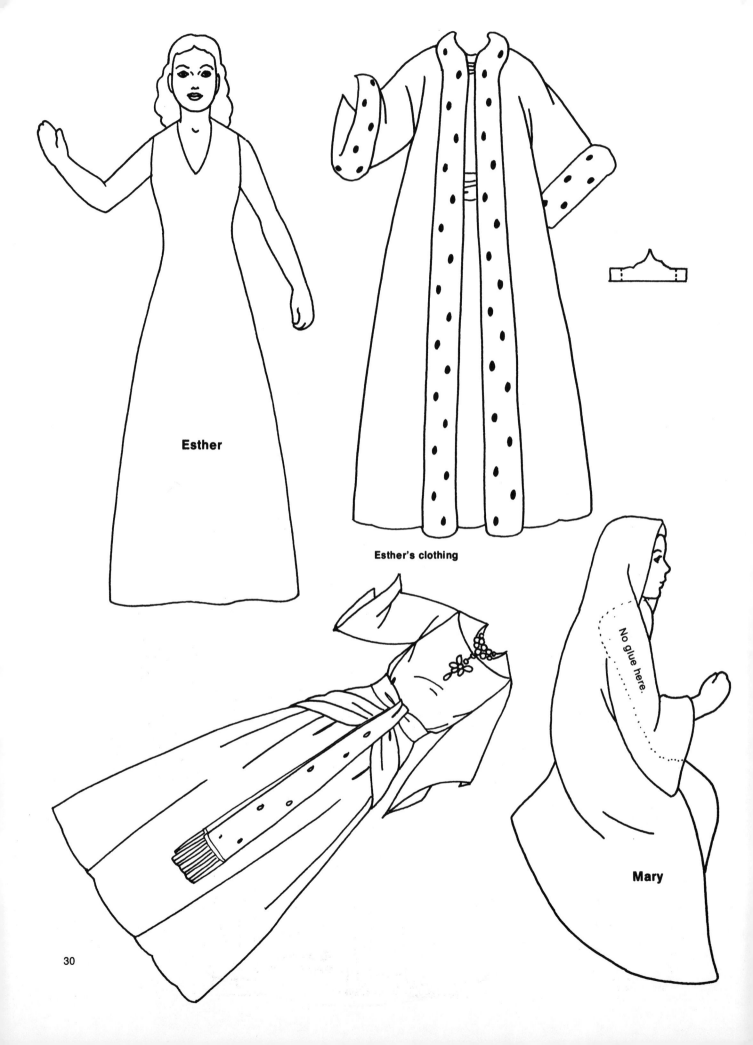

Esther

Esther's clothing

No glue here.

Mary

30

Wise-man's crown
Cut 2.

Clip here.

for baby Jesus doll

baby Jesus

fisherman

fisherman

Going to
Bethlehem

31

NEW TESTAMENT PROJECTS

The Promised Savior

Isaiah 7:14, 15; 9:6, 7; Micah 5:2; Matthew 1:18—2:6

Materials needed:
Gold paper
Construction paper—yellow, black (2)
Tagboard
Crayons, felt-tip pens, or tempera paints
Glue
Brass paper fastener

Directions:
Cut one star out of gold paper and one from yellow construction paper. (See page 31 for patterns.) Glue these together. Cut baby Jesus figure from tagboard and color. Glue baby to center of black construction paper. Attach star to cover baby, using a brass paper fastener. Glue second sheet of black construction paper to back of first sheet.

Going to Bethlehem

Luke 2:1-5

Materials needed:
Construction paper—tan or brown
Tagboard
Yarn—tan or brown
Tempera paints or felt-tip pens
Glue

Directions:
Draw the map (next column) on tan or brown construction paper. Punch holes as indicated. Cut figure of Mary, Joseph, and donkey (pattern on page 31) from tagboard and add color. Glue a 20-inch piece of tan or brown yarn (to match background) on the back of the completed figure (see

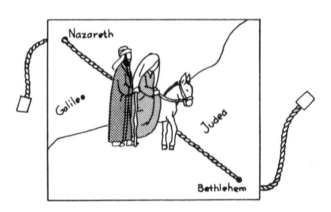

pattern for angle). Thread one end of yarn into each hole. Glue paper tags to ends of yarn. Now glue a second sheet of construction paper to back of first to strengthen it. Make sure yarn can be moved freely. Mary, Joseph, and donkey will "walk" from Nazareth to Bethlehem as you tell the story.

Baby Jesus Is Born

Luke 2:1-7

Materials needed:
Construction paper—black, brown, gray, tan, white yellow
Tagboard
Brass paper fastener
Felt-tip pens or tempera paints
Glue

Directions:
Cut two doors (page 48) from brown construction paper. Cut one piece of brown the size of both doors to make back wall of stable. Glue this to a piece of black paper. Fold doors on dotted lines

and glue to sides. Cut hinges and handles from black paper and glue in place. (Or, these could be added with paint or pens.)

Cut animals from appropriate shades of construction paper. Use patterns from Noah project. Cut slivers of yellow construction paper and glue on "floor" of stable to represent hay. Glue animals in position.

Cut figure of Mary, her arms, and baby Jesus (use patterns on pages 31 and 48) from tagboard. Add color to figures. Slip Mary's arms through slit in figure and hold in place with paper fastener. Glue figure of Jesus in Mary's arms. Now position figures in stable and add glue around edges of figure. Make sure that Mary's arms move freely. If you wish to make this more durable, glue a second piece of black paper to back.

Baby Jesus in the Manger

Luke 2:6, 7

Materials needed:
Craft sticks (4)
Heavy cardboard
Tagboard
Glue
Outing flannel—
  5-inch square
Tempera paints

Directions:

Make baby Jesus figure using pattern on page 31. Add color. Glue two sets of craft sticks together as shown in sketch. Cut a piece of heavy cardboard 5 inches by 4 inches. Score and fold across the middle of the 4-inch width. (Or use a double thickness of tagboard.) Glue crossed sticks ½ inch from each end of manger trough. When dry, paint manger with brown tempera paint. Use dry grass, straw, or raffia for hay. Glue in place. Wrap baby in square of soft cloth, tie with yarn if you wish, and place in the manger. Or, if you prefer a larger, 3-D baby Jesus, use the directions that follow to make a baby Jesus doll.

Baby Jesus Doll

Materials needed:
Facial tissue
Cotton

Yarn
Cloth—flesh color,
  and a pastel
Felt-tip pens
Glue

Directions:

Mold cotton to approximate shape shown in sketch. Cover this with a facial tissue. Hold tissue in at neck, waist, and wrists by tying small pieces of yarn around these areas. Trim hands and bottom of garment. Add flesh-colored paint to "hands." Cut a circle of the flesh-colored cloth. Glue this to head to form face. To make cloth fit head, snip into cloth and overlap around edges. Glue short pieces of black or brown yarn on head for hair. Add features with felt-tip pens. Cut a blanket, about 8 inches square. Turn down one corner of blanket and place this over baby's head and tie around neck with a piece of yarn. Wrap blanket around baby.

Wise-man

Matthew 2:1-12

Materials needed:
Construction paper—bright color
Facial tissues
Glue
Gold paper
Chenille wires
Sequins or glitter

Directions:

Cut a semicircle of construction paper, about 4¾ inches in diameter. Cut a ½-inch semicircular hole for neck. Roll the semicircle into a cone shape and glue or tape in place. Roll a facial tissue into a tight ball and place in the center of another tissue. Gather this and twist to form the head and neck. Coat with glue and set aside to dry. When dry, color face and head with felt-tip pens or tempera paints. Glue the neck into the hole at the top of the cone. When dry, twist a chenille wire (about 8 inches) around the neck to form arms. Glue to hold in place. Turn up ends for hands. Drape another tissue over the head and glue. Cut the crown out of gold paper or yellow construction paper, glue together to fit head, and glue in place over tissue. Sequins or other decorations may be added to crown. Gold braid or rickrack could also be added to Wise-man's robe. If you want a richer look, cover semicircle with fancy wrapping paper and use a silky cloth for the headdress.

The Wise-men's Gifts

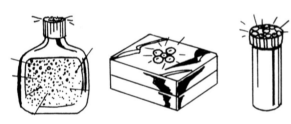

Materials needed:
Small plastic shampoo bottle
Small pill bottle
Small gift box
Gold spray paint
Gold paper
Glue
Glitter—gold and another color
Sequins or other decorations
Cologne, incense

Directions:

Spray paint the small shampoo bottle and the pill bottle (one with a lid that comes off easily). Allow to dry. Cover box with gold paper (or spray paint). Glue sequins to top of box and lid of pill box. Glue colorful glitter to sides and lid of shampoo bottle. Or decorate any way you wish. Fill pill bottle with incense, shampoo bottle with cologne (watered down), and place gold glitter in box. These can represent the expensive gifts the Wise-men brought the baby Jesus.

The Journey to Egypt

Matthew 2:13-23

Materials needed:
Construction paper—gray or brown, white
Tagboard
Crayons, felt-tip pens, or tempera paints
Glue
Chenille wires

Directions:

Cut two baby Jesus figures (page 31) from tagboard and glue together. When dry, color figure. Cut two of Mary figure (page 30) from white construction paper. Color each of these (one facing left, one facing right). Make donkey according to directions on page 9. Glue Mary figure together at top (make sure you leave area free of glue as shown on pattern) and on either side of donkey. When glue is dry, baby Jesus can be inserted in Mary's arms or removed. Make Joseph figure according to directions for lame man, page 45, using the pattern on page 61.

John the Baptist

Mark 1:1-8

Materials needed:
Tagboard
Crayons, felt-tip
  pens, or tempera
  paints
Chenille wire
Glue
Woolly material
Leather strip
  (shoelace, or strip
  of chamois, etc.)

Directions:

Make figure of John from tagboard, using the pattern on page 22. Color both front and back. While figure is drying, cut two garments from the woolly material. (Remember to turn pattern over for second piece.) Glue these to front and back of figure. Cut a thin strip from leather (or use a leather shoelace) to tie around figure's waist.

The Boy Jesus in the Temple

Luke 2:41-51

Materials needed:

Construction paper—black (3)
Acetate—clear
Felt-tip pens (permanent ink)
Masking tape
Stapler

Directions:

Place a sheet of clear acetate over your pattern (made from pattern on page 49) and tape both to the table so they can't move. Color the areas with many colors, then make heavy black lines to look like lead. Cut gothic window design in three sheets of black paper. (Cut on dotted lines of pattern.) Staple the acetate to one piece of paper and trim paper and acetate to fit inside other paper (at least ½ inch smaller on all sides). Now glue this between the other two sheets of black. Add a thread hanger and place in a window.

The Nobleman's Son

John 4:46-54

Materials needed:

Construction paper—two colors

Tagboard
Crayons, felt-tip pens, or tempera paints
Glue

Directions:

Cut boy and leg (page 49) from tagboard. Glue together and color. Cut bed (page 51) from construction paper and glue at bottom, sides, and pillow, leaving top of bed open. The boy can lie down, sit up, and walk. The children will enjoy playing with him after you have told the story.

Jesus Calls Four Fishermen

Matthew 4:18-22

Materials needed:

Construction paper—deep blue
Clear acetate—red, green, yellow
Yarn or cord—natural color (about 100 inches)
Paper reinforcements
Felt-tip pen (black, permanent ink)
Stapler

Directions:

Cut a fish and fin out of each color of acetate (patterns on page 50). Fold each fin in half along

dotted line of pattern. Fit each fin against the lower part of a fish, with the pointed part of fins toward tail. Fasten in place with two staples (see sketch), then fold fin down and over staples. Mark eyes and other lines with permanent-ink felt-tip pen.

Punch five holes on each long side of blue construction paper. Stick paper reinforcements around back of holes. Lace a long piece of yarn or lightweight cord back and forth, from bottom to top, as you do a shoe, and tie a bow at the top. Glue a second piece of construction paper to the back to strengthen craft. Fish can be tucked under the yarn. Use this as a craft with the story mentioned above, or with any of the stories of Jesus and His fishermen helpers.

On the Sea of Galilee

Materials needed:
Construction paper—dark blue and brown
Tagboard
Glue
Stapler (optional)
Acetate—clear and scraps of colors
Felt-tip pens or tempera paints
Chenille wire—blue
Nylon mesh bag

Directions:
Mark waves on one sheet of blue construction paper. Cut a 1-inch frame from second piece. Cut one sheet of clear acetate to fit under frame (about 8 inches by 11 inches). Cut the boat "track" in the acetate (see sketch). Now glue or staple acetate on top of waves and add the blue frame to this.

Cut as many fish (page 48) as you want from various shades of acetate. (You may want to glue some of these beneath the acetate before gluing base

together.) Cut a 4-inch square of nylon mesh bag for fishing net. Cut figures of men (page 31) from tagboard and add details with pens or tempera. Cut two boats (page 48) from brown construction paper and glue together with figures of men inside. Cut blue chenille wire into two 3-inch pieces. Fold each in half. Bend up cut ends and glue one on each side of boat. These will slip beneath the acetate so boat can slide down "track" easily.

Slip chenille wires beneath acetate so boat rests on "track." Place fish on net and gather edges of net together. The ends may be glued to the hands of the fishermen, or may be held in place with Plasti-Tak after fishermen have "caught" fish. If you want a more substantial net, cut a circle of the nylon mesh, 5 or 6 inches in diameter, and run a length of yarn around the edge as a drawstring. Pull this up as tightly as you wish after fish have been placed in net.

Jesus Heals a Sick Man

Mark 2:1-12

Materials needed:
Construction paper—white, dark color
Tagboard
Crayons, felt-tip pens, or tempera paints
Glue
Yarn

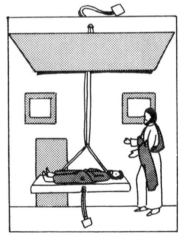

Directions:
Fold down a 2-inch section of a sheet of white construction paper. This will be the roof section. Proceed to draw and color a door and windows as in sketch. Color folded-down part also. Cut a small hole in center of fold.

Cut man, leg, and bed (pages 50 and 52) from tagboard and color. Attach man's leg with a paper fastener. He will be able to lie down, stand, and walk. Glue two 12-inch pieces of yarn to back of bed (see sketch). Knot yarn together just above bed. Glue house to second sheet of construction paper. Punch a hole in this sheet just above the hole in the fold. Now thread the yarn up through these holes and glue a paper tag to the ends of the yarn. Glue another sheet to back of the scene. (Make sure yarn can be pulled easily.)

If you want to use this as a visual, make a Jesus figure to go with the figure of the sick man. Also, if you have some, glue pictures of Bible-times people to the background to simulate a large crowd in the house. (Look in old visuals paks for pictures.)

Jesus Forgives a Woman

Luke 7:36-50

Materials needed:
Construction paper—any color
Tagboard
Tempera paints or felt-tip pens
Brass paper fastener
Yarn
Glue

Directions:
Cut figure of woman, two of her arms, and figure of Jesus (page 52) from tagboard. Add color with paints or pens. Cut two pieces of yarn (black or dark brown) in 8-inch lengths. Fold yarn in half and glue to woman's head. Tie hair together at neckline with a scrap of yarn. Secure arms to figure (one on either side of body) with paper fastener. Glue hair between her hands. Glue figures of Jesus and the woman to the background. Leave glue off around woman's arms so they move freely. Cut the alabaster box from a scrap of pink paper, or color it pink. Glue in place. Glue a second sheet of construction paper to back of project.

Jesus Heals a Servant

Matthew 8:5-13

Materials needed:
Construction paper—white, a color
Crayons, felt-tip pens, or tempera paints
Glue

Directions:
Cut the two figures (page 51) from white construction paper and add color. Cut two of the sliding door and glue together. Fold back tab and glue together. Now glue the standing figure to the door, with tab to left. Cut a slit in background paper, 6½ inches long. Add the figure of the sick man to the background, to left of slit. Put door through slit, then glue a second piece to back of background, gluing only around edges. Now, at the appropriate time in the story, the door can be pulled out to show that the man is well.

Jesus Stills a Storm

Mark 4:35-41

Materials needed:
Construction paper—blue, dark blue, brown, white
Glue
Brass paper fastener
Crayons or tempera paints

Directions:
Draw and cut boat and mast (patterns on page 53). Use brown or black paper. Cut waves from dark blue paper as shown. Edge with white tempera paint or crayons. Cut figure of Jesus from white paper and add color. Add a tab to His left hand. Cut sail from white paper. Cut strips of water from dark blue paper and slit as shown.

Glue boat, mast, sail, and water to background paper. Leave top of boat and top of water open so

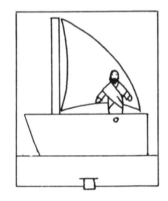

animated pieces will work. With a brass paper fastener, attach figure of Jesus to boat, toward stern. Now insert waves beneath water so that tab comes through slit in water.

Jesus should be down in the boat, sleeping, when the story begins. As the storm hits, waves come up, then Jesus rises, calms the sea, and waves disappear.

Peter Walks to Jesus on the Sea

Matthew 14:22-33

Materials needed:
Styrofoam trays
Crayons, tempera paints, or felt-tip pens
  (permanent ink)
Tagboard
Chenille wires

Directions:
From tagboard, cut two figures of Peter and two of Jesus (page 54). Bend two 12-inch chenille wires in half and glue one to Peter's figure and one to Jesus' figure. Leave about 1 inch of the wires extending below each foot. Glue second figure on top of each of these. Add color to figures. Cut a free-

form piece of Styrofoam (about 6 inches by 4 inches) for each figure. Punch small holes in each piece of Styrofoam where feet will touch the tray. Insert chenille wires through holes and bend over, front ones one way and back ones the opposite direction. Figures will now float on water.

The figure of Jesus, without the Styrofoam base, can be made to be used in other stories.

Jairus' Daughter

Mark 5:22-24, 35-42

Materials needed:
Tagboard
Construction paper
Crayons, felt-tip pens, or tempera paints
Fabric (optional)

Directions:
Cut the little girl (page 49) from tagboard and add color. Cut bed (page 51) from construction paper and color. Glue bed to large sheet of construction paper, being careful to apply glue only where indicated on pattern (solid line). The little girl can lie down in bed, sit up, and kneel beside her bed to say thank-you to God. (She will stay in this position if you slip a portion of her hair under the open part of the pillow.)

For a touch 'n feel picture, cover bed with fabric.

Jesus Walks on the Sea

John 6:16-21

Materials needed:
Construction paper—dark blue, green or tan
Acetate—clear
Chenille wire—dark blue
Glue
Tempera paints

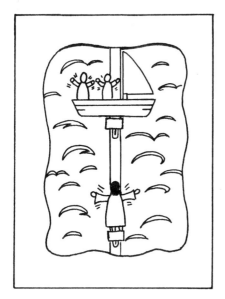

Cotton ball (optional)
Stapler and staples

Directions:

Cut ½-inch strips from one side of two sheets of dark blue construction paper. Glue the two strips together and set aside. Paint waves on one blue sheet and let dry. Cut acetate to about 7½ inches by 10 inches. Staple this over the sheet with the waves.

From tagboard, cut two boats and masts, two of the Jesus figure, and four to six of the disciple figure (patterns on page 52). Cut one pair of arms for each two figures. Color with tempera paints. Make faces on half the figures, and color the backs a solid color. Cut two pieces of blue chenille wire, 2½ inches each, and fold each in half. These will be inserted in boat and Jesus figure, allowing about ¾ inch of tabs to extend below figures. Now glue figures of men together, leaving space as indicated for arms to be slipped in position. Glue boats and masts together, leaving space at top of boat where disciples can be added. Cut sail from tagboard, fold on dotted line, fit fold around mast, and glue.

Make two rings of blue paper, about ½ inch wide, and long enough to fit around the long double blue strip. Slide these onto the strip and staple ends of strip in position on "sea." Glue second sheet of blue on bottom of this. Cut a piece of tan paper to fit base. Cut out a free-form shoreline and glue over base (see sketch).

Now bend chenille wire tabs (on boat and on Jesus) and glue to the two rings of paper on the long strip. Slip disciples into boat. Optional: Glue cotton around boat and Jesus figure for waves.

As you tell the story, have the boat at shore closest to you. Have figure of Jesus folded down and covered with your hand. Move boat out to sea, rocking it as you talk about the storm. Then lift and move the figure of Jesus and have Him walk on the sea.

Jesus Heals a Deaf Man

Mark 7:31-37

Materials needed:
Tagboard
Crayons, felt-tip pens, or tempera paints
Yarn—red
Glue
Construction paper—any color

Directions:

Cut the face and two tongues (page 55) from tagboard. Color with crayons, pens, or paints. Insert a 4-inch piece of red yarn between tongues and glue together. Punch holes where indicated in ears. Cut the slit in the upper lip and insert the tongue. Thread yarn through hole in lower lip and let extend below beard. Put glue around entire head except where yarn extends. Place on a sheet of construction paper. Make sure yarn can move freely. Children can do as Jesus did and place their fingers in the man's ears and touch his tongue as they role play the story.

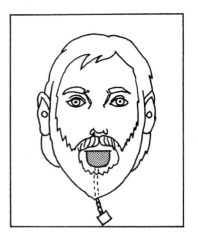

The Good Samaritan

Luke 10:25-37

Materials needed:
Construction paper—white, green, brown, gray
Brass paper fastener
Crayons, felt-tip pens, or tempera paints
Glue

Directions:

From brown or gray construction paper, make a donkey using pattern on page 54. Cut the two figures and the extra arm (page 54) from white construction paper. Color both. Attach the arm to the good Samaritan with a brass paper fastener. Mount finished figures on a green or brown background, with the donkey behind the men. Add a road, rocks, a few scrubby trees, etc., if you wish.

If you want a more substantial visual, punch paper fastener through figure and background, then glue a second sheet on the back.

The Prodigal Son

Luke 15:11-32

Materials needed:
Construction paper—dark green or tan, white
Brass paper fastener
Crayons, felt-tip pens, or tempera paints

Directions:

Cut figures (page 56) from white construction paper and color. Glue to background sheet—either dark green or tan. Add a road and small bushes. Fasten arm at proper place with a paper fastener. Glue a second sheet to back for extra strength.

A Little Lamb

Materials needed:
Quilt batting
Tagboard
Glue
Brass paper fastener
Felt-tip pens

Directions:

Cut a body (no legs) and head from tagboard. (Patterns on page 56.) Attach body to head with a paper fastener. Cut two bodies with legs, and two heads from the quilt batting. Glue these to both sides of tagboard body and head. Glue legs together. Add facial features and hooves with felt-tip pens. Add a small yarn bow if you want.

This little lamb can be used with the story of the lost lamb (Luke 15:3-7) or as a craft whenever an animal is needed.

Blind Bartimeus

Mark 10:46-52

Materials needed:
Construction paper—white
Crayons, felt-tip pens, or tempera paints
Clear adhesive-backed plastic
Black marker—washable ink

On plastic cover, draw black eye sockets with a washable-ink felt-tip pen.

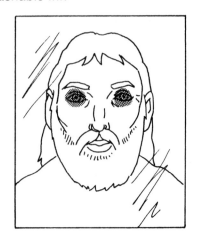

Directions:

Trace blind man's face (page 58) on white construction paper and color. Show his eyes open here. Now cover entire picture with the clear plastic. On top of plastic, with *washable* felt-tip pen, draw black holes over eyes. In the story, as you tell how Jesus made mud to cover Bartimeus' eyes, mix a little water with some dirt and cover the black eye sockets. Then wipe with a facial tissue. The black will come off with the mud and the man's open eyes will show. If the children are making their own to take home, give each one a tiny plastic sandwich bag of soil and a tissue to complete their craft. Help them add the black sockets before taking home the craft to show their families.

Zaccheus

Luke 19:1-10

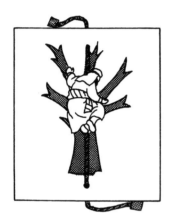

Materials needed:

Construction paper—green, brown
Tagboard
Felt-tip pens, crayons, or tempera paints
Yarn—brown
Glue

Directions:

Cut tree out of brown construction paper, and figure of Zaccheus (page 57) from tagboard. Add color to figure. Glue tree to piece of green construction paper. Punch small holes 1 inch from top and 1 inch from bottom as shown. Glue figure to center of 20-inch piece of brown yarn. Thread ends of yarn through holes at top and bottom of green background. Glue another sheet of green construction paper to back, leaving small spaces open at top and bottom for yarn to pass through. Add paper tags to ends of yarn. Help Zaccheus climb the tree to see Jesus.

Jesus Loves All Children

Materials needed:

Construction paper—blue, white
Tagboard
Tempera paints, crayons, or felt-tip pens
Brass paper fastener

Directions:

Cut two circles 7½ inches in diameter, from the white construction paper. Cut a tagboard cross and add color. Draw the map, shown above, on one circle and color. Glue circles together, with cross between circles. Cut children and head of Jesus (pages 56 and 57) from tagboard and color. (Cut a boy figure for a boy, etc.) Glue these around the edges of the finished circle. Fasten circle to a sheet of blue construction paper with a paper fastener. Glue head of Jesus over fastener. Then glue another sheet to back of this one.

This could be a class project by letting each child work on one figure. If there are more children, let them make a large map for the classroom, or simply make a larger circle and have more little figures around the edge.

The People Praise Jesus

Matthew 21:1-11

Materials needed:

Construction paper—tan and various colors
Tagboard
Tempera paints or felt-tip pens
Yarn—tan
Glue
Cloth scraps (optional)

Directions:

Cut as many garments as you want, using a variety of colors of construction paper. Or, for a more interesting effect, use cloth scraps for the garments. Glue garments to page (see sketch).

Cut figure of Jesus (page 60) from tagboard. Add color. From tagboard, cut a donkey, using pattern on page 23. Cut a slit for his mouth and add yarn reins. When dry, glue figure of Jesus to donkey. Glue a 20-inch piece of tan yarn diagonally across donkey's back.

Punch holes in paper as illustrated. Thread ends of yarn through holes. Glue a second piece of construction paper to back of completed page for added strength. Leave glue off corners so yarn can be pulled freely. Glue paper tags to ends of yarn.

Jesus Died on the Cross

Mark 15:21-39

Materials needed:
Acetate—clear red
Aqua Podge (a clear decoupage finish)
Evergreens—flat variety
Thread

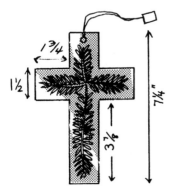

Directions:

Make a pattern of a cross, using the dimensions given in the sketch. With your pattern, cut a cross from the clear red acetate. Glue some flat evergreens on one side of the cross, using the Aqua Podge, then cover the cross and the evergreens thoroughly with another coat of the liquid. Punch a hole in the top and tie a length of thread to the cross. Hang in a window or use as a mobile.

A Cross Wallhanging

Materials needed:
Construction paper—light green
Tempera paints
Glue
Tagboard
Empty glue bottle (optional)

Directions:

Cut two crosses (page 59) from the construction paper and one from the tagboard. Trace the lilies onto one paper cross. Glue one paper cross to each side of the tagboard cross. Paint the lilies. Glue a yarn loop to the top of the back of the cross for hanging.

If you prefer, a small flower container can be made by cutting off the top of a glue bottle, covering it with the green paper, and gluing it to the back of the cross. This can be filled with water and a small vine or flower can be kept fresh to represent the new life offered through the resurrection of Jesus.

Jesus Lives!

Matthew 28:1-10

Materials needed:
Construction paper—black, gray, yellow, white
Glue

Crayons, tempera paints, or felt-tip pens

Directions:

Cut the angel (page 60) out of white construction paper and add color. Cut the stone from gray paper. Cut a piece of yellow slightly smaller than the gray stone. This will be the opening of the tomb. Cut a ¾-inch strip from the long side of the black construction paper. Put glue on one edge of the strip and glue to the paper as shown in the sketch. Make sure the upper edge of the strip is loose from background. Glue the yellow piece in the center of the background, just above the strip. Glue the angel on the yellow piece. Now place the gray stone so it will role in the slot made by the strip.

Use this as a visual to tell the resurrection story, or as a craft for that lesson.

Stained-Glass Fish

Materials needed:
Waxed paper
Crayons
Construction paper—black
Masking tape
Newspapers
Iron

Directions:

Cut a piece of waxed paper, 9 inches by 12 inches. Fold in half to make a picture 6 inches by 9

inches. Place one half of the waxed paper over the pattern of the fish (made from page 60) and secure both to the table with masking tape. With crayons, fill in the fish, and divide the background into sections and fill in with color. Go over all lines with a heavy black crayon line to look like lead. Remove masking tape and fold the other end of the waxed paper over the colored area, place between several layers of newspaper, and press with a warm iron. This will seal in the color and cause the waxed paper layers to stick together. Cut two frames 7 inches by 10 inches, and 1 inch wide. Glue the stained-glass design between the two frames. Punch two small holes in the frame and hang with thread. Place in a bright window.

Use this with the story of the breakfast with Jesus on the seashore (John 21:1-17), or with any story about fish or fishermen.

Jesus Goes Back to Heaven

Matthew 28:16-20; Acts 1:6-11

Materials needed:
Construction paper—blue, white
Tagboard
Yarn—blue
Crayons, felt-tip pens, or tempera paints

Directions:

Trace the pattern of Jesus (page 61) onto tagboard. Add color. Punch two holes in the blue paper as shown. Glue center of a 20-inch piece of yarn to back of the figure of Jesus. Thread ends of yarn through holes. Add paper tags to ends of yarn. Cut cloud from white paper. Glue top and side edges of cloud to background as shown. Jesus will ascend to Heaven when you pull the yarn. Glue second piece of paper to back, making sure yarn can be pulled easily.

The Lame Man Who Walked

Acts 3:1-10

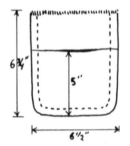

Materials needed:
Tagboard
Glue
Chenille wires
Brass paper fastener
Tempera paints or felt-tip pens

Directions:

Cut two each of the lame man figure and his arm (page 61). Add color. Also cut two bases, 2 inches square. Glue corresponding pieces of body together, inserting two 4-inch chenille wires from waist down through the feet, allowing 1 inch to extend beyond feet. Insert these in two holes punched in one base. Bend wires in opposite directions. Glue on other base to bottom. Glue arms together and attach with the paper fastener. Make a staff from chenille wire.

Have the man lying down until he is healed, then he can stand. Children can pretend to be Peter and raise the man onto his feet. This can also be used for the story of Paul's healing the lame man at Lystra (Acts 14:8-20).

Ananias and Sapphira

Acts 5:1-11

Materials needed:
Unbleached muslin (or old sheet)
Glue
Yarn
Cardboard
Crayons

Directions:

Make cardboard patterns following diagram above. Using pieces of unbleached muslin or an old sheet, cut two of the full pattern and one of the half pattern. Glue the large pieces around sides and bottom. Glue the half section on top of this, on sides and bottom. Allow to dry thoroughly. Now turn bag right side out. You will have a bag with a special pocket inside. Punch holes around top as indicated. Cut two or three pieces of yarn, 24 inches each. Put glue on one end of each piece and twist together to make a large point. Run this through holes and tie a knot in each set of ends.

Make as many coins as you want by cutting circles (1½ to 2 inches in diameter) from cardboard and coloring them gold or silver. Use this as a visual by placing one or two coins in the special pocket to represent the money Ananias and Sapphira lied about to the Holy Spirit. Let the children use this to role play the story when you have told it. The money-bag could also be used with other stories, such as the selling of Joseph or the betrayal of Jesus.

The Apostles in Prison

Acts 9:17-42

Materials needed:
Construction paper—black, brown or gray
Tagboard
Glue
Brass paper fastener
Tempera paints, crayons, or felt-tip pens

Directions:

Cut from the tagboard one of each figure (page 62) and add color. From black construction paper

45

cut twelve strips for the prison bars, ½ inch by 9 inches each, and four strips each ½ inch by 7 inches. Glue the long strips together by two's. Then lay these double strips down evenly, with a short strip at top and one at bottom. Glue ends. Then glue second strips on top of the short strips. Make a double strip, 2 inches by ½ inch, for the latch. Glue left edge of prison door to a piece of brown or gray construction paper. Attach latch with the paper fastener to hold right side of door, as shown. Slip figures behind bars in such a way that they can't slip out. This can be used for the story of Paul and Silas (Acts 16:16-40) if you explain that their feet were in stocks.

Paul Escapes in a Basket

Acts 9:22-25

Materials needed:
Construction paper—brown or gray
Tagboard
Crayons, felt-tip pens, or tempera paints
Yarn (to match wall)
Glue

Directions:
Cut basket and figure (page 61) from tagboard. Add color. Punch holes in handle and at bottom of bas-

ket, as indicated. Fold a piece of brown construction paper into sixteen squares so creases will look like blocks in the wall. Or, draw irregular blocks with a black marker. Thread a 16-inch piece of yarn through holes and glue ends to back of brown paper at top and at bottom. Glue a second piece of paper on back of this. Basket should slide up and down easily.

Dorcas, a Kind Woman

Acts 9:36-42

Materials needed:
Construction paper—various colors
Tagboard
Crayons, felt-tip pens, or tempera paints
Glue
Cloth scraps
   (optional)

Directions:
Cut the figure of Dorcas (page 61) from tagboard and add color. Cut clothing from various colors of construction paper. Or, use scraps of cloth for the clothing. Glue Dorcas to the center of a piece of construction paper leaving her right arm free to hold the garments. If you want, make a paper doll or two, glue on outing flannel underwear, and make cloth or felt garments that will adhere to the flannel. Let the children take turns changing the clothing on the doll.

Peter and the Angel

Acts 12:1-17

Materials needed:
Chenille wires—black
Tagboard
Crayons
Yarn—black

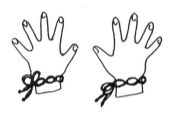

Directions:

Help the children draw around their own hands and wrists on the tagboard. Let them color and cut these out. Bend chenille wire in half and twist together about every inch to look like iron links. Make sure the last link is twisted securely. Take 16 inches of yarn, fold in half, and knot at both ends. Thread this through the first and last links of the chain and tie in a bow.

Let the children pretend to be Peter and have the chains tied together around their wrists. The "angel" can untie the chains. When the children are finished with their role play, have them put the chains around their tagboard wrists and glue the hands and wrists to a piece of construction paper.

Paul Is Shipwrecked

Acts 27:13-44

Materials needed:

Construction paper—dark blue, black, brown, white, gray
Crayons, felt-tip pens, or tempera paints
Glue
Yarn
Tagboard

Directions:

Cut the figure of Paul (page 62) from tagboard. Add color. Cut two of the angel from white con-

struction paper. Add color. Cut rocks from gray paper, boat from brown, sail from white (patterns on page 53), and cloud from gray or black. Use dark blue for the background. Glue boat at bottom and ends. Glue mast and sail to background. Glue an 18-inch piece of yarn to back of angel. Thread yarn through holes punched at top left of the background and just below top of boat. Glue paper tabs to ends of yarn. Glue on cloud at top and left side. Angel will now descend from cloud to boat, and back. Figure of Paul can be inserted into boat. Glue rocks at front of boat. You may want to add a bundle of dried grass to Paul's hand, as though he is throwing out wheat. Other items, such as bundles and anchors, could be placed in the boat to be cast out by the children after you tell the story.

A Bible Scroll

Materials needed:

Cardboard rod from pants hanger
Craft sticks (2)
Construction paper—white, yellow, or natural
Yarn
Glue
Tempera paint or crayons

Directions:

Cut rod into two pieces, 7 inches each. Cut two craft sticks in half. Glue one piece into each end of the two cardboard rolls. Color sticks brown. Cut a strip of construction paper, 6¾ inches by 10 inches, and glue one end around each cardboard roll. Print a memory verse inside the scroll. (Remember that scrolls were held out horizontally, not vertically.) If the children are going to be writing inside their own scrolls, let them glue in pieces of lined newsprint to make it easier to print. Roll both sides toward the middle and tie with a double piece of yarn (with knots tied in ends).

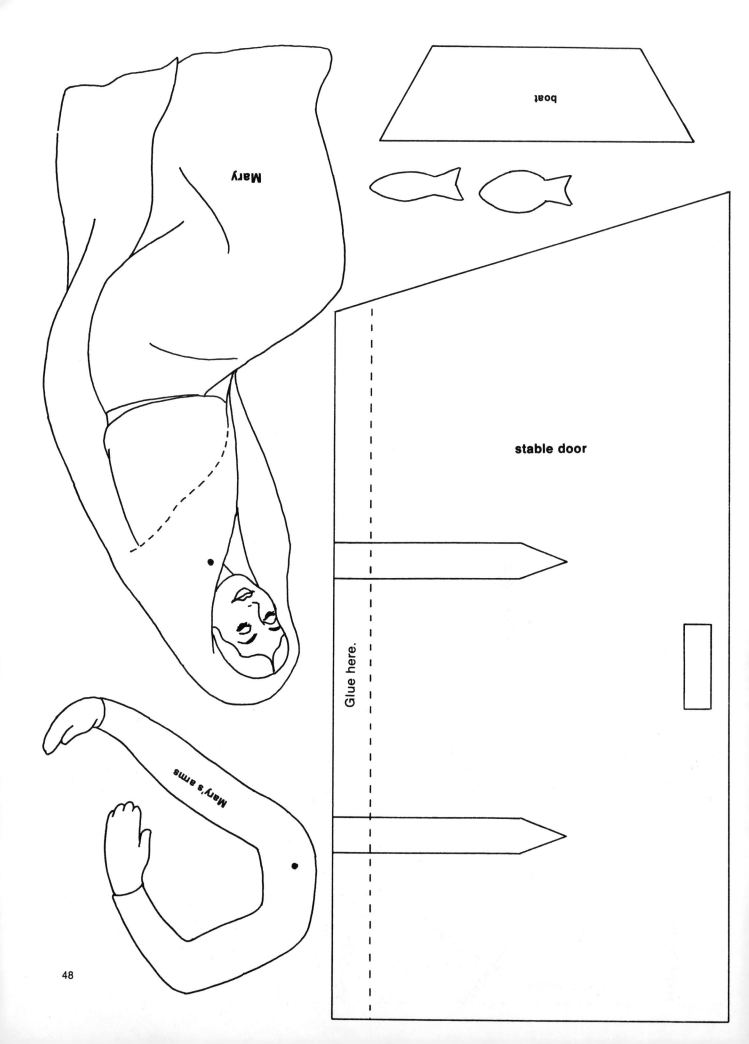

boat

Mary

stable door

Glue here.

Mary's arms

48

Cut on dotted line for frame.

sick boy

Jairus' daughter

the boy Jesus

49

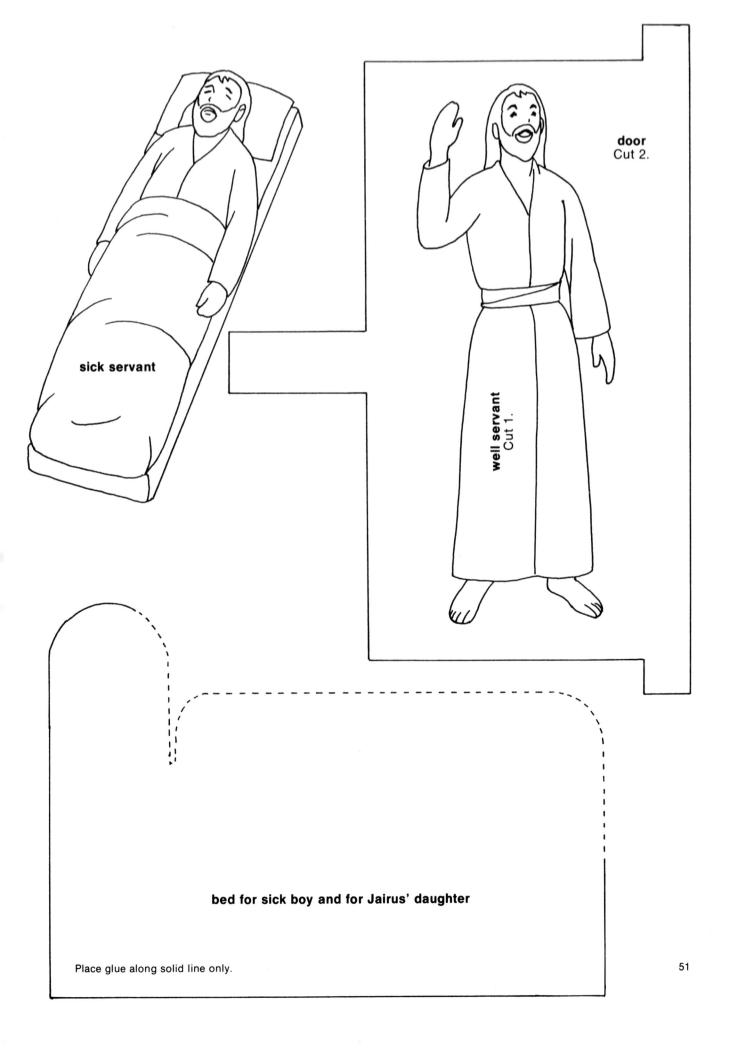

sick servant

door
Cut 2.

well servant
Cut 1.

bed for sick boy and for Jairus' daughter

Place glue along solid line only.

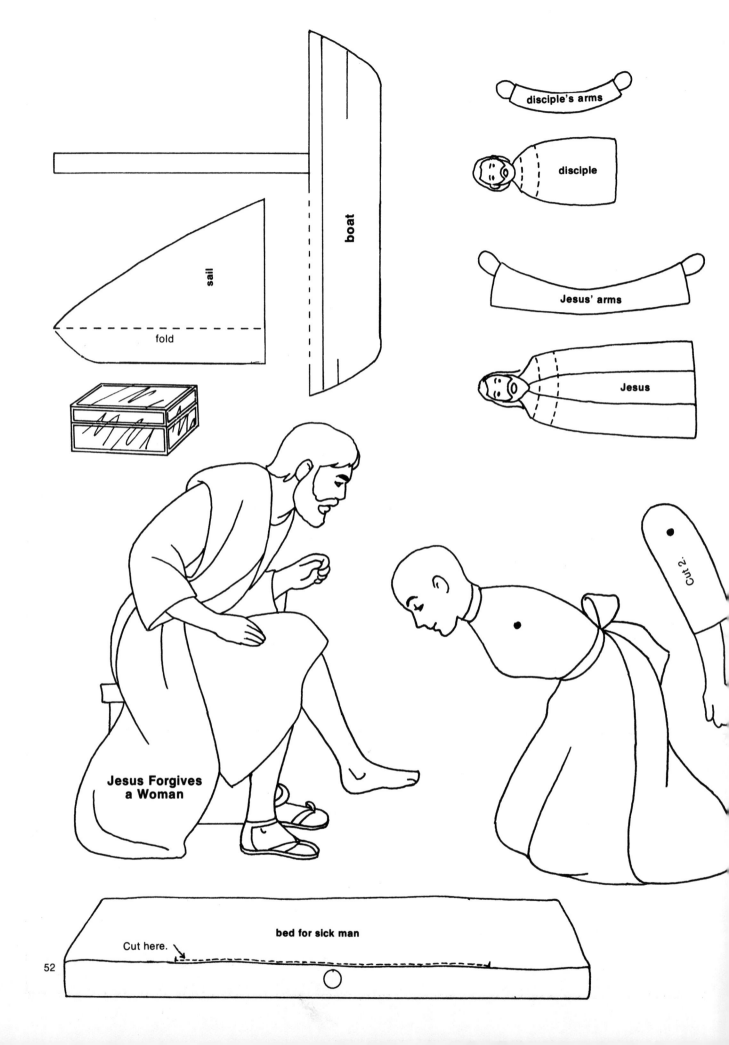

disciple's arms

disciple

Jesus' arms

Jesus

sail

fold

boat

Cut 2.

Jesus Forgives
a Woman

bed for sick man

Cut here.

52

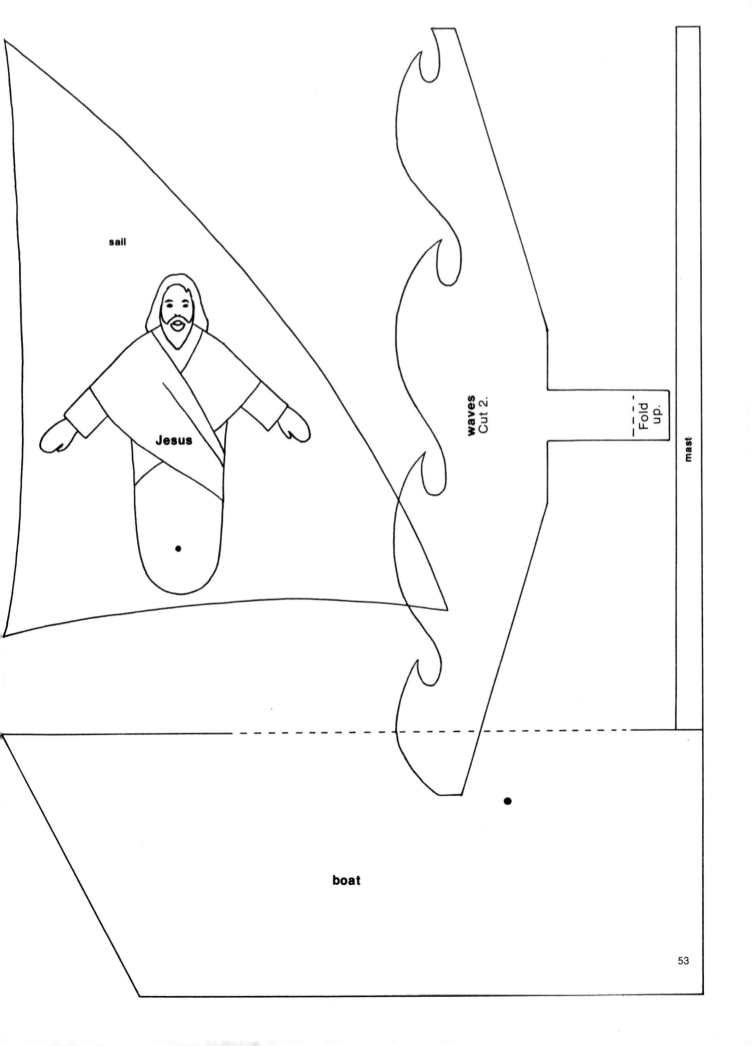

sail

Jesus

waves
Cut 2.

Fold
up.

mast

boat

53

Peter

Jesus

good Samaritan

54

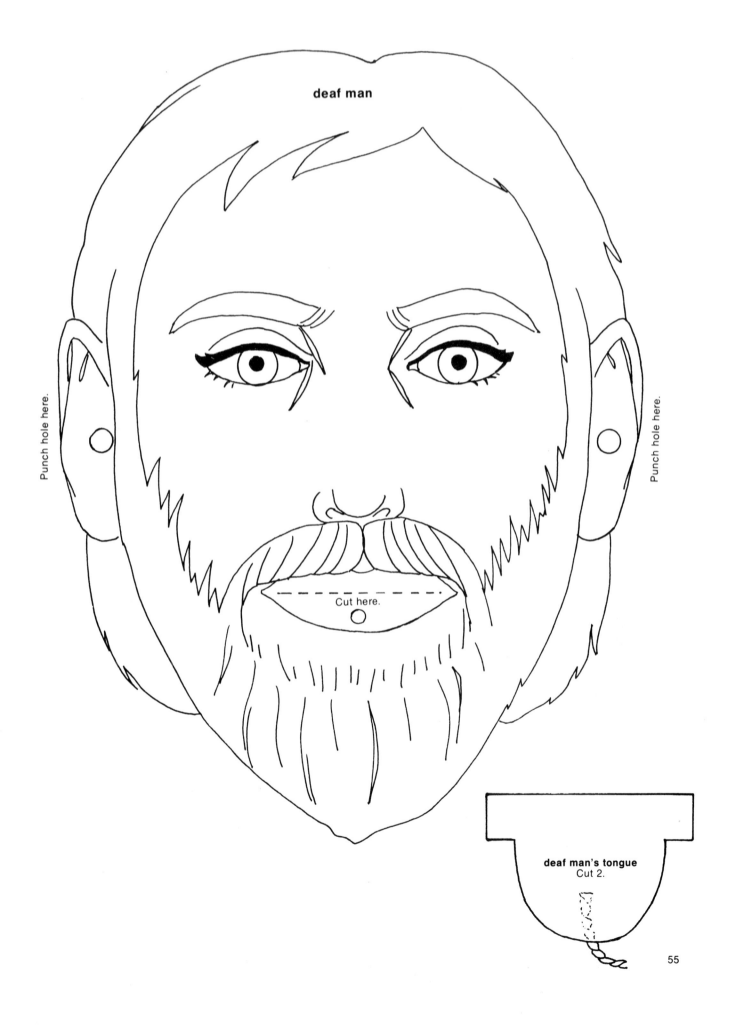

deaf man

Punch hole here.

Punch hole here.

Cut here.

deaf man's tongue
Cut 2.

55

father's arm

lamb's head

prodigal son

lamb

Cut either a boy or a girl for each child.

Zaccheus

Jesus' head

blind man

garment

garment

for Cross Wallhanging

garment

59

for The People Praise Jesus

stone

angel

Stained-Glass Fish

Place on fold.

palm branch

60

arm for lame man

Jesus Goes Back
to Heaven

Dorcas

Paul

Joseph and
lame man

61

angel

Paul

for The Apostles in Prison

OTHER CRAFT BOOKS FOR YOUR LIBRARY

CRAFT ITEMS

Jumbo Chenille Wire (6390; $3.50; 100 pieces, 12", assorted colors)
Craft Sticks (6388; $3.95; 1,000 sticks)
Plasti-Tak (7100; $1.25)
Brass Paper Fasteners (6298; $1.35; 50 pieces)
Scissors (6238—pointed; $11.40 per dozen; 6237—rounded; $11.40 per dozen)
Evertite Glue (6397, $3.40, pint; 6298, $4.65, quart)
Construction Paper (6261; $1.95; 50 sheets, assorted colors)
Artist Brushes Assortment (6272; $2.25; 20 brushes, sizes 1-5)
Happy Day Crayons (6221, $.49, 8 colors; 6222, $.79, 16 colors)
Wipe-Off Crayons (6223; $.45, 8 colors)

All prices subject to change without notice.